A Pocketful of Words

Some Short Poems

Rebekah Crilly

BookLeaf
Publishing

India | USA | UK

Presentation by *BookLeaf Publishing*

Web: www.bookleafpub.com

E-mail: info@bookleafpub.com

ISBN: 9789358363722

First edition 2021

"I wish to dedicate this to anyone who's never quite found their place in this world. This one is for you. Let's find it together."

Acknowledgements

To my 5th form geography teacher who once scrawled over an exam paper "this is not an English essay", I am forever grateful for this compliment even if it was intended as an insult. Life is an English essay, my friend. To the Lord for blessing me with the written word even when my mouth fails me. To my brothers and sisters, mother and father: all the love I possess in this world has come from you. To my boys for loving me more than I deserve. And to wine. You are behind the majority of these words.

Preface

This short collection of poetry comes to you from a myriad of places; some light and fluffy, and some rather painful. Beyond that, there is no discernible theme or pattern to observe. No great meaning to unpack or puzzle to solve. These poems are simply an expression of those niggling thoughts that won't fizzle out until they are written down and neatly packed away. It is hoped that whoever finds this book upon their lap can derive some comfort from these words; even if it's just a smidgen of the comfort I felt in writing them.

HAPPY HOUR

Sometimes all there is

is wine and tea

and the vacuum of time

that exists between

for such little hands

they possess such power

ruling my senses

by minute, by hour

the leaf soothes me in all its goodness

the vine wraps me

in its numbing juices

of which hour I shan't say

it is now half past

I trade my tired mug
in

for a tall glass

RESTLESS

She took the day off to rest

but all she could do was count

all the things that needed done

from twenty down to one

would the rags wash themselves

chance would be a fine thing

would the unsightly find a home

as if by magic on their own

and herein this feeble verse

lay exactly what was wrong with rest

the truth that no such thing exists

only nudges and
prompts impossible to
resist

A SILENT SORT OF SORROW

Words were her only solace

though only in writing never spoken

the sound of voices too loud

for a quiet heart now broken

to speak does no good

such a deafening blow

send the pain into the void

of where the verses flow

the cadence of the sentence

as it forms itself on pages

reveals the long-held secrets

of whispering birds in cages

the written truth remains

for everyone to see

as your talk turns to ashes

lost in a distant breeze

as long as I have my wits

and words find themselves flowing

allow me to forever write my sorrows

and keep my mouth unopen

PERSPECTIVE

Life was hard

wasn't there a softer version

a spongey marshmallow type

without all the edges

like bumpers in the bowling alley

that cushion the blow

steer you in the right direction

keep you from the gutters

a beginner's level

even intermediate

like Super Mario

with all the clouds and extra lives

coins for the taking

the worst of it

life was not hard

there were clouds

she had some coins

she was nowhere near the gutters

LINES

If lines told a story

what would they speak

would they tell of laughter

or nights of lost sleep

what would the crow's feet

at the eyes disclose

would they whisper smiles

or tales of woe

the lines are inevitable

but by your design

you are the author

who dictates each line

OH WORRY

Oh Worry, how could I have been so foolish

to think you were a friend

after all this time and all your failings

my farewells I'm afraid I must send

your constant reminders of what could go wrong

I will certainly not pine

your what ifs will no longer seduce me

your doubts I will no longer call mine

oh Worry, you most certainly were a foe

it is now as clear as is the day

and while the wind will shake the trees

for you I will no longer sway

I've since found Gratitude and Hope

I do believe you know them

I'll send them your regards

though they warn you are not welcome

ELEPHANTS FOR SALE

Help! a family of elephants

has taken up residency inside my head

they thud and stomp

cause all sorts of ruckus

my wits are reaching their end

wouldn't they be happier in the wild

part of a herd or even the local zoo

but they seem to prefer

my cerebrum to grass

leaving my gray matter rather blue

don't get me wrong

I like elephants as much as the next guy

but with no sign of cessation

even Attenborough himself

has declared the family

an unprecedented infestation

call pest control

enlist the circus

these mammoths must be silenced

for my poor brow can take no more

and would much prefer the quiet

HOLE IN A FENCE

In my dream last night

we watched a footage of you

how bizarre

footage of footage

you picked a hole in a fence

big enough to clamber through

we cheered and clapped

as if we understood

I see now

with such perfect clarity

what you were trying to do

Heaven awaited

and with that on
the other side

wouldn't we all
tear through

THE SUNDAY EFFECT

The new week brought hope

opportunity for growth

today. Sunday.

a day of hangover inspired oaths

I solemnly declare the end

of our weekend affair

this is harder for me I mutter

through the bottle I stare

it was a long thirty seconds

as I paced the
kitchen floor

reheating the last
slice

vowing no more

LITTLE LEGOS

Tiny blocks of bold colour

masked in every corner

plotting their next attack

on some unsuspecting mother

torturous drops of rainbow

as if fallen from the skies

could innocent boys plot such mischief

behind my watchful eyes

but on days like today

when I feel a little frayed

each pinch serves as a reminder

the blocks aren't there to stay

for there will come a day when

my now treacherous floor is bare

and I'll wish with all my heart

the LEGOs were still there

A SPACEMAN'S MONOLOGUE

I was destined for greatness

beyond infinity, among the stars

the painful truth was

I'd never make it that far

no intergalactic mission

my ship never reached the moon

instead I'd find myself confined

to a solitary room

Sharpie engraved on my sole

if not a Space Ranger, who was I

what were these wings for

if they would
never get to fly

I would never
meet the Alliance

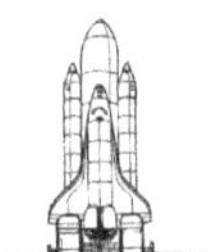

I would never
defeat the evil
Zurg

but I found I could live on Earth

if it meant being his world

DICK AND ANNE

Love me the way Dick loves Anne

as he walks her to the bus stop

and takes her hand

not the way Romeo loved Juliet

too messy and poisonous

though love me no less

love me the way Dick loves Anne

an unassuming sort of love

peaceful and calm

not the way Heathcliff loved Cathy

too haunting and drawn out

though love me as fiercely

love me the way Dick loves Anne

quiet and gentle

like a sea sweeps the sand

not the way Cleopatra loved Antony

too tragic and volatile

though love me eternally

so take my hand

walk me to the bus stop

and love me the way Dick loves Anne

BYE BYE BIRDIE

And just like that

you were snuffed out in your prime

I hope you weren't headed somewhere

someone waiting

and you didn't appear on time

and now they think you're rude

for standing them up that morning

never knowing how you were taken

without reason or warning

you lay so peaceful

not a blemish or mark to be found

as though you just dropped from the sky

without making a sound

fly on little bird to your heavenly home

without breakage or halt

and if I see your friend

I'll explain it wasn't your fault

ANOTHER BITTER WIFE

My husband is having an affair

with not one but eleven men

how can I compete

with a difference of ten

if only he'd be subtle

and at least try to hide

but he continues to flaunt

forty three inches wide

poetry in motion

the beautiful game

there's a few other words

I'd use to
describe the
same

I wonder if I
choked and
died

would he
notice at all

and in case it wasn't clear by now

I don't like football

INTO THE WILD

When all else fails

and everyone seems to disappoint

escape to the wild to let it all out

scream at the trees

the branches will trap your yells

confide in the flowers

their petals will never tell

take off your shoes

long grass between your toes

and let Mother Nature

soothe your weary soul

cry sore at
the sky

as barefoot
you stand

the earth can
endure

much more than people can

A SNAIL AND HIS SHELL

Behold The Snail and his travelling
show

see how he carries a home on his back

without a flinch, such effortless motion

no other bug can boast such an act

Extraordinary Feats of the Mini Beast

they travelled far and wide to see

and for only one human penny

though the snail performed for free

for The Spider they came in their hordes

observed his design, how he traps the
fly

for The Butterfly they gasped in awe

her flutter would instantaneously mystify

even The Stick Insect and his tired
routine

The Cricket and his now familiar sound

garnered more interest, a louder
applause

than anything The Snail ever found

and so he retired from the public eye

with a heavy heart and heavier shell

though no one would miss him much

the tale of The Snail no one would tell

the saddest
part that he
couldn't forget

his failed
attempt at
fame

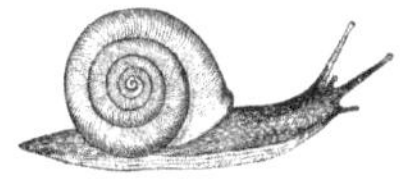

though long
forgotten

among the swarms

for him his shell would never feel the
same

THE SUNFLOWER

She willed her sunflower to grow tall

to make up for her own shortcomings

and so she watered it daily

in the evening and in the morning

grow tall it did like Jack's beanstalk

blooming yellow above the town

until one day in a frenzy

she tore the flower down

such overwhelming beauty

how could she hope to compare

and so all that
lay left

were shreds of
sunflower
everywhere

MEN IN SHORTS

All year long

they wear their shorts with pride

unfaced by whatever weather

may greet their legs outside

cargo, athletic, floral

more often than not the same pair

these men defy logic - the cold

but mind not to stare

were their knees their best feature

it was hard to say

perhaps all of their trousers

were simply in the wash that day

was it a bold statement

me not cold. me man

or maybe just an attempt

to work on their tan

whatever the reason for such a move

we salute you

your bravery

and of course your lovely legs too

THIRTEEN QUESTIONS

I'd ask her how the weather is

and if her hands still hurt

I'd ask her if Heaven has snowdrops

and if she saw me at my worst

I'd ask her if Granddad was tall again

and did he still sit next to you

I'd probably be silly and ask

if Elvis is up there too

I'd ask her if she still plays Boggle

and makes peas with mash potato

I'd ask her if she has a secret garden

for all her flowers to grow

I'd ask her if He forgives me

and if there is any room

I'd ask her if she'd help me get there

though prayed it would not be soon

THE END

Rocks pebbles and gems

fell in clusters from the sky

and the people cried

the end is nigh

no swarms of locusts

or rivers turned red

only raining stones

smacking their heads

though dodge they tried

they could not escape

for it was already written

their   crushing
fate

TROUBLE

There's this wonderful expression

my mother likes to say

if trouble is to come, it will

don't meet it half way

I'll admit I've become accustomed

to meeting it in the middle

greeting it with a hug

and inviting it in for dinner

instead of waiting for the wolf

to blow the house down

I'll poke it and prod it

willing it to come around

so Trouble, if I must meet you at all

can I meet you when you are here

not when you are far away

unseen

not even near